STO

ACPL ITEM
DISCARDED

D1616259

EAST

‹GERMANY›

PLACES AND PEOPLES OF THE WORLD

EAST GERMANY

David McKenna

CHELSEA HOUSE PUBLISHERS
New York • New Haven • Philadelphia

PP26-006087

Library of Congress Cataloging-In-Publication Data

McKenna, David.
East Germany.
Includes index.

Summary: Surveys the history, topography, people,
and culture of East Germany, with an emphasis on its
current economy, industry, and place in the political world.

1. Germany (East). [1. Germany (East)]
I. Title.
DD280.6.M35   1987   943.1   87-11619

ISBN 1-55546-197-2

1 3 5 7 9 8 6 4 2

Editor: Rafaela Ellis
Associate Editor: Melissa Padovani
Copy Editor: Crystal G. Norris
Art Director: Anita Noble
Designers: Carol Molyneaux, Adriana Kulczycky, Wilbur Davidson
Production Manager: Brian A. Shulik
Editorial Assistant: Wendy Cox
Series Advisor: Rebecca Stefoff

COVER: Leipzig, East Germany's second largest city, has been
a center of culture for 800 years. The East German flag
flies over its town hall.

◂CONTENTS▸

DENMARK

BALTIC SEA

Rügen Island

Stralsund

Pomeranian Bay

• Rostock

Wismar

Schweriner See

Kummerower See

Müritz See

Plauer See

Oder R.

GERMAN DEMOCRATIC REPUBLIC

FEDERAL REPUBLIC OF GERMANY

EAST BERLIN

West Berlin

Frankfurt

• Magdeburg

Elbe R.

Spree R.

• Halle

• Leipzig

Harz Mts.

• Dresden

Neisse R.

• Erfurt

• Karl Marx City

Ore Mts.

CZECHOSLOVAKIA

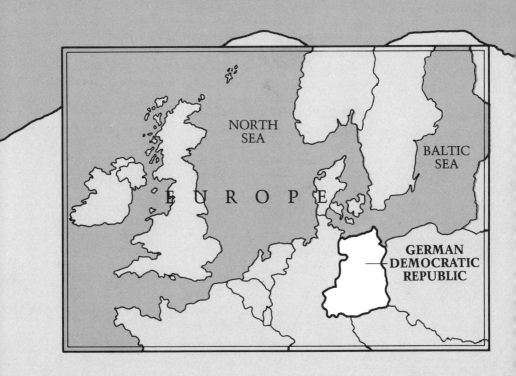

NORTH
SEA

BALTIC
SEA

E U R O P E

GERMAN
DEMOCRATIC
REPUBLIC

POLAND

N

Land and People

Area	41,766 square miles (108,592 square kilometers)
Highest Point	Ore Mountains, 3,900 feet (1,170 meters)
Baltic Sea Coastline	199 miles (320 kilometers)
Capital	East Berlin (population 1,200,000)
Other Major Cities	Leipzig (population 550,000), Dresden (population 520,000), Karl Marx City (population 320,000), Magdeburg (population 290,000), Rostock (population 235,000), Halle (population 232,000), Erfurt (population 212,000)
Population	16,900,000
Population Density	404 people per square mile (156 per square km)
Population Distribution	Urban, 75 percent; rural, 25 percent
Official Language	German
Major Ethnic Groups	German (Teutonic), about 10,246,500; Sorbs, about 100,000; Jews, about 3,500
Religions	Christian (mostly Lutheran), 63.4 percent; atheist, 11.4 percent; nonreligious, 25.2 percent; other, less than 1 percent

Economy

Resources	Lignite (soft coal), potash, rock salt
Imports	Petroleum products and fuel, iron ore, cobalt, uranium, copper

Agriculture	Supplies 90 percent of GDR's food and employs 9 percent of work force; 98 percent state-owned
Major Crops	Wheat, oats, fruits, sugar beets, vegetables
Industry	Accounts for 70 percent of national income and employs more than 40 percent of work force; 98 percent state-owned
Major Industries	Coal mining, chemical production (including plastics and fibers), microelectronics, appliances
Currency	GDR mark, equal to about U.S. 37 cents
Average Annual Income per Couple	Equal to U.S. $7,800

Government

Form of Government	Communist state controlled by the Socialist Union party (SED)
Head of State	Erich Honecker, first secretary of the SED
Prime Minister	Willi Stoph, chairman of the cabinet
Governmental Bodies	The Politburo, a committee of 18 SED members that directs national policy; the People's Chamber, whose 500 members and president are appointed by the SED; Council of Ministers, a 44-member assembly appointed by the SED; the Council of State, a 25-member committee made up of members of Parliament
Minority Political Parties	Christian Democratic union (CDU), Democratic Farmers party (DBD), Liberal Democratic party (LDPD), National Democratic party (NDPD)
Administrative Organization	15 districts, each with a parliament and assemblies for counties, towns, and villages

◄HISTORY AT A GLANCE►

by 1000 B.C.	Teutonic tribes have settled in the hills and lowlands of central Europe. These related tribes include the Franks, Thuringians, Saxons, Lombards, Bavarians, Goths, Vandals, Angles, and Jutes.
100 to 1 B.C.	Teutonic tribes moving south and west clash with the expansion of the Roman Empire to the north and west. The area along the Rhine and Danube rivers becomes the frontier between the two peoples. The Romans call the land to the north of the frontier Germania.
100 through 200s A.D.	Germanic tribes advance across the frontier and into the central provinces of the Roman Empire.
476	The Germans dethrone Romulus Augustulus, the last emperor of the Western Roman Empire. The Saxons settle in Britain, the Lombards in Italy, and the Franks in France.
500 through 1700s	The various Germanic kingdoms are part of the Christian Holy Roman Empire. Powerful independent states—Bavaria, Saxony, and others—emerge within Germany. German politics are characterized by particularism: the pursuit of their own ends by individual dukes and princes rather than obedience to a strong central ruler.
800	After conquering most neighboring Germanic kingdoms, Frankish king Charlemagne is crowned holy Roman emperor by Pope Leo III.
936	Otto I assumes the throne of the German and Holy Roman empires and begins an era of Saxon rule.

1024	The Salian dynasty from the northern Rhine region takes power from the Saxons.
1122	A 47-year war between the monarchy and the Roman Catholic church ends with the failure of the Salian dynasty. The princes are now more powerful than the emperor.
1155 to 1190	The Holy Roman Empire is ruled by the German king Frederick I, or Barbarossa.
1200 through 1400s	Prominent families, including the Hapsburgs, Luxembourgs, and Wittlesbachs, control large parts of the Germanic Empire.
1517	Martin Luther begins his protest against the Roman Catholic church in Wittenberg, eastern Germany. His reformist ideas give rise to the Protestant movement.
1618 to 1648	The Thirty Years' War between Protestants and Catholics starts in Germany and spreads to other European nations. It leaves Germany devastated and impoverished. Many independent dukedoms form, including Prussia in northern Germany.
mid-1700s	Frederick William the Great, king of Prussia, conquers many neighboring states and builds a large, well-trained army.
early 1800s	The Napoleonic Wars rage through Europe and destroy the remnants of the Holy Roman Empire. Napoleon conquers most of Germany, including Prussia, and reorganizes it as the Confederation of the Rhine.
1815	Prussian forces help Great Britain defeat Napoleon at Waterloo. Germany reorganizes into a new confederation of 38 states, each with its own ruler and constitution.
mid-1840s	The lower and middle classes begin to demand reforms in government and greater political power.
1848	The German states try to form a National Assembly in Frankfurt, but Prussia refuses to participate. The

statesman Otto von Bismarck rises to power in Prussia and launches a military campaign to bring all of Germany under Prussian leadership.

1871   Prussia is the dominant force in central Europe and includes two-thirds of the German territory. William I is named *kaiser,* or emperor, of a new German Empire, and Bismarck becomes chancellor.

1914   Germany enters World War I with the hope of conquering Russia, France, and other European nations.

1918   The tide of war turns against Germany. In November, Germany surrenders. A postwar government called the Weimar Republic is set up, but it lacks the confidence of the German people and faces severe problems of economic depression and lack of unity.

1918 to 1932   During its 14-year life, the Weimar Republic undergoes 20 changes of government. Some new political parties—including the National Socialists, or Nazis—promise to restore the nation to world power.

1933   Under the leadership of Adolf Hitler, the Nazis seize control of the German government and begin a period of military rule called the Third Reich. One of the greatest horrors of the Reich is the mass imprisonment and extermination of millions of Jews, Gypsies, and other peoples in concentration camps.

1939   Germany invades Poland, setting off World War II.

1943   At the turning point of the war, Russia defeats the Germans at Stalingrad and forces them to retreat.

1944   The United States and Great Britain attack the German forces occupying France. The Russians continue to attack Germany from the east.

1945   The German war effort grinds to a halt. Hitler commits suicide, and Germany surrenders to the Allies a week later.

1945 to 1949   The victorious Allies (France, the United States, Great Britain, and the Soviet Union) divide Germany into two independent nations: the Federal Republic of Germany (West Germany), supervised by the United States, France, and Great Britain, and the German Democratic Republic (East Germany), managed by the Soviet Union. The capital city of Berlin is divided between the two nations, although it lies inside East Germany.

1946 to early 1960s The GDR is governed by the Soviets and by Russian-trained Germans. Russia gradually turns control of the country over to German leaders. The Berlin Wall is built to prevent East Germans from escaping to the West.

1971 Several agreements between East Germany and Western nations slightly ease restrictions on travel, trade, and communications.

1973 East and West Germany pledge to respect each other's borders. Both join the United Nations.

late 1970s East Germany renews its strong ties to the Soviet Union and the Communist system of government.

1984 Forty thousand East Germans are allowed to emigrate to the West—the greatest number since the building of the Berlin Wall.

currently Erich Honecker governs East Germany as first secretary of the Socialist Unity party (SED). Relations between East and West Germany appear stable.

EAST
‹GERMANY›

Despite economic and industrial progress, East Germany retains its Old World charm.

East Germany and the World

The German Democratic Republic (GDR), commonly known as East Germany, was established in 1949, yet it was once part of one of Europe's oldest nations. Its craggy hills were settled by the Franks, Saxons, Vandals, and other fierce Teutonic tribes that migrated south from Scandinavia in about 1000 B.C. Since then, the area that is now East Germany has faced violence and upheaval, but it has also been the seat of great artistic and intellectual achievement. Conquerors, philosophers, dictators, and composers have all flourished in Germany. It has been home to people as diverse as Martin Luther and Adolf Hitler. And along the way, its turbulent and fascinating history has affected the history of the entire world.

Today, East Germany continues to affect the world. Created after World War II, when Germany was divided into two nations, it is now part of the global struggle between the Communist and non-Communist views of the world. The other half of the divided nation, now called the Federal Republic of Germany (or West Germany), is allied with the United States and other Western nations. East Germany is a Communist country. Its social and political systems were established by the Soviet Union, which gained control over the country in the wake of World War II.

Although the Soviets have relinquished direct control over East Germany, their structure continues to govern the country's political and social life. As in the Soviet Union, there is no private ownership in the GDR. Instead, the East German people collectively own all corporations and public property, which the government strictly supervises in the name of the people. The government also tightly controls the news media, forbids most travel to the West, and must approve all artistic and literary products. The state decides who will go to college and what they will study once they get there.

Yet, despite these restrictions, the East German people have one of the highest standards of living in Eastern Europe. East Germany's factories produce sophisticated electronic equipment and heavy machinery, and its huge collective farms provide 90 percent of the food needed to feed its people. Jobs are plentiful, housing is available and affordable, and consumer luxuries such as television sets and automobiles are becoming more and more available. Furthermore, the state pays for schooling, health care, day care for the children of working mothers, and pensions for the elderly and the disabled.

Nevertheless, some 3.5 million East Germans, most of them young and well educated, fled the country for the West between 1949 and 1960. In 1961, the East German government constructed the Berlin Wall, a steel

The government has built modern apartments to provide housing for all East Germans.

and concrete barrier separating the divided city of Berlin so that East Germans could not cross into democratic West Berlin. The flow of East Germans out of the country was greatly reduced, but the damage had already been done. So many young men left the country that, today, one in five East Germans is of retirement age, and women greatly outnumber men.

The East Germans have dealt with this lopsided population problem by restructuring their society. State and volunteer organizations help the elderly, and the state helps women in the work force by providing them with equal pay for equal work, as well as maternity and child care assistance. The government also trains all people—male and female—to be productive members of East German society.

In recent years, the GDR government has made overtures to the West. Trade with Western nations has increased, and Western visitors are welcomed into the country. At home, many restrictions have been eased. For example, religion, once strongly discouraged, may now be practiced freely. Nevertheless, relations with the Soviet Union remain strong, and East Germany continues to hold good standing in the Communist bloc (a group of nations aligned with the Soviets).

Many of the most important events in the history of our world have shaped or been shaped by Germany. Both democracy and communism have their roots there. Classical music, literature, and philosophy all thrived in its ancient cities. The rise and fall of the Roman Empire, the cultural achievements of the Renaissance, and the world-molding events of World Wars I and II are entwined with German history. Although life in East Germany has changed drastically since it became a separate nation almost 40 years ago, its people remain proud of their ancient heritage and their many cultural achievements. Despite their Communist government and Socialist lifestyle, they remain Germans, heirs to the proud Teutonic tradition.

Although it was once heavily forested, the East German countryside is now used as farmland. In fact, almost half of the country's land is used for growing food.

The Land

The German Democratic Republic lies in the heart of the northern European plains, bounded on the west and southwest by West Germany, on the east by Poland, on the southeast by Czechoslovakia, and on the north by the Baltic Sea. About the size of the state of Alabama, it covers 41,766 square miles (108,592 square kilometers)—making it slightly less than half the size of West Germany. Its capital city, East Berlin, occupies 165 square miles (429 sq km).

The west-southwestern border, which divides East Germany from West Germany, is 857 miles (1,380 kilometers) long. It is the GDR's longest and most closely watched frontier, a place where military patrols, barbed-wire fences, and minefields separate East from West. The southeastern border that separates East Germany from Czechoslovakia extends for about 265 miles (427 km) along the Ore Mountains. The 261-mile (412-km) eastern border, which divides the country from Poland, follows the Neisse and Oder rivers, then veers to the west just before the Oder reaches the Baltic Sea. The northern boundary extends for about 199 miles (320 km) along the Baltic coast. Just off the coast lies the huge island of Rügen, a popular tourist resort.

East Germany lies across two geographic zones: the Northern Lowland and the Central Uplands. The Northern Lowland occupies about 80 percent of the land and includes the coastal, northern, and central plains regions. Its gravelly, sandy plains were formed by glaciers that moved slowly through central Europe many thousands of years ago. Although the Elbe and Oder river systems flow across the plains, they do not cut into them very deeply; therefore, the region has no hills higher than 330 feet (99 meters).

As it moves southward, the Northern Lowland gradually rises into the Central Uplands. This zone consists mainly of huge rock masses, the remains of ancient mountains worn down over the ages. Shifts in the earth's crust formed East Germany's highest mountain range, the Ore, where summits rise to 3,900 feet (1,170 meters). This area's other mountain chains, the Harz and the Thüringer Wald, are also composed of rock masses that have eroded over thousands of years. These areas are heavily wooded and contain deposits of potash, rocksalt, lignite (soft coal), and some other minerals. The lower hills of the Thüringer Wald and Ore Mountains form basins and then descend into the Elbe Valley lowlands near the city of Dresden.

Rivers and Lakes

The Elbe and the Oder are the country's two major rivers. The Elbe River flows northwest from East Germany into West Germany and then into the North Sea. It has three principal tributaries—the Saale, the Havel, and the Spree. The Oder River begins in the Czechoslovakian mountains and flows north into the Baltic Sea. Along with its principal tributary, the Western Neisse, it forms the East German-Czechoslovakian border.

The Northern Lowland contains an area called the Mecklenburg Lake Plateau, where many marshes, ponds, and small lakes are located. These waterways were created in the same way as the area's other land features—by the huge ice formations that moved through the region thousands of years ago. The largest of these glacial lakes is the Müritz See (Müritz Sea). Others include the Kummerower See, the Schweriner See, and the Plauer See.

The flat central plains region was formed in prehistoric times by glaciers.

Climate

Overall, East Germany's climate is temperate. But the weather varies greatly throughout its different geographic zones. The nation's average temperatures range from about 32° Fahrenheit (0° Centigrade) in January to 65°F (18°C) in July. Annual rainfall averages between 24 and 25 inches (610 and 635 millimeters) and increases during the summer.

In the Central Uplands, temperatures are lower than the national average, and rainfall is higher. Some sections of the Harz mountain region average 58.4 inches (1,460 millimeters) of rain per year, whereas the basins are relatively dry. In the central lowlands, seasonal temperature variations are less extreme and rainfall is lower. The coastal climate is most representative of the country. There, temperatures and rainfall are about equal to the national average.

Plants and Animals

Because of East Germany's dense population and long history of cultivation and construction, little natural vegetation remains. The thick forests that once covered its hills have been cleared, and many of them have been replanted with different types of trees.

In the Northern Lowland, for example, forests of beech, oak, and birch have vanished. In some areas, these natural forests have been replanted with pine trees. The lowland's marshy areas, once teeming with forests of alder trees (a type of birch whose bark can be used to make a dye), now maintain only boggy grasslands. The lush forests of broadleaf oak and beech that once blanketed the Central Uplands disappeared long ago. Although some beech forests still remain in the mountain regions, most have been replaced by planted conifers (pine trees). In the highest elevations, beech and silver fir trees grow.

Long-billed white storks strut along East Germany's seacoasts and waterways.

Almost half of East Germany's total land area is used to cultivate food crops. In the southern regions, as much as 75 percent of the land is planted. Wheat, sugar beets, rye, and potatoes are the chief crops. Wine grapes are grown in the southeast.

Like its plant life, most of East Germany's animals are part of its agricultural industry—dairy cattle and hogs are the most common. The destruction of East Germany's vast forestland greatly decreased the number and variety of animals. Today, the only animal that really thrives in East Germany is the deer. Red and roe species of deer, common throughout Europe, abound in the East German mountains. Some wild boar live deep in the forests. In remote areas, a few bears, wolves, foxes, otters, badgers, and wildcats can also be found.

Despite its long Baltic Sea coast, East Germany does not have a wide variety of fish and marine life. Herring, mackerel, and cod live in the coastal waters, and some species of freshwater fish swim in the Northern Lowland's ponds and rivers. Some species of birds thrive along the GDR's waterways. The most notable of these are the sea eagle and the white stork. Other bird life disappeared years ago along with the forests.

The revolution of 1848 was a turning point in East Germany's history.

Ancient
Teutonic Tribes

Archaeological evidence indicates that the German people are descended from the ancient Teutonic tribes that migrated to central and northeastern Europe from Scandinavia in about 1000 B.C. These tribes—the Franks, Thuringians, Saxons, Lombards, Bavarians, Goths, Vandals, Angles, and Jutes—lived in the glacial hills and lowlands between the Rhine and Oder rivers. Primarily an agricultural people, these early Germans built small villages of log homes and farmed communal land plots. Their government was one of the first democracies. Councils of freemen made all government decisions, except in times of war, when military leaders ruled.

During the 1st century B.C., the powerful Roman Empire, under the leadership of Julius Caesar, began to expand its influence from the Mediterranean Sea into western and northern Europe. At the same time, many Teutonic tribes began to move west and south. The two forces clashed in what is today known as the Rhine and Danube river region, and the area became a frontier between the two opposing empires. For the next three centuries, fierce battles raged. During this period, the Romans built the *limes*, a 3,000-mile (4,830-kilometer) series of fortifications along the frontier. They named the land across the limes "Germania."

By the 2nd and 3rd centuries A.D., Germanic warriors had weakened Roman power along the Rhine-Danube frontier and had advanced past the

limes toward the heart of the Western Roman Empire. When these warriors dethroned Roman emperor Romulus Augustulus in 476, the Western
Roman Empire collapsed. The most powerful Germanic tribes then
divided the fallen empire's territories, which included most of western
Europe. The Angles and the Saxons settled in what is now Britain, the
Visigoths in modern-day Spain, the Lombards in the northern and central
regions of what is now Italy, and the Franks in Gaul (ancient France).

The Frankish Dynasty

After Rome's collapse, the Franks began conquering neighboring territories and quickly became the most powerful of the Germanic tribes. They
overtook the German lands along the middle and lower Rhine, and in 481,
the Frankish king Clovis I established the Merovingian Dynasty in the
region. During his reign, which lasted until 511, the Franks adopted many
Roman customs and beliefs, including Christianity. In 496, Clovis con-
verted to Roman Catholicism, an act that gained him the support of Gaul's
powerful Christian clergy and strengthened his reign.

After King Clovis's death in 511, a series of ineffective monarchs
weakened the Franks' authority. Over the next two centuries, the kingdom
became increasingly disunited and vulnerable to attack, particularly from
the other Germanic tribes who had lost land to the Franks during Clovis's
reign. But its power was restored in 751, when Pepin the Short unified the
Frankish kingdom as the Carolingian Empire.

The Carolingian Empire

Upon Pepin's death in 768, his kingdom was divided between his two
sons, Carloman and Charles. After Carloman died in 771, Charles became
the sole king of the Frankish empire. Under his reign, the empire
expanded greatly. He became known as Charles the Great, or
Charlemagne.

For 30 years, Charlemagne ruthlessly attacked neighboring kingdoms, subjecting them to Carolingian rule and converting them to Chris-

tianity. He conquered the Lombards, the Avars, and the Bavarians. On Christmas Day in 800, Pope Leo III crowned Charlemagne the Holy Roman emperor.

Charlemagne and his son, Louis the Pious (who succeeded him to the throne in 814) not only increased the size of their empire but established an effective, centralized government as well. They built a feudal society in which land ownership and political and social status were based on a hierarchy, or class system. They cleared forests and built roads and bridges to advance agriculture and commerce. And they encouraged education, art, and literature to flourish.

After Louis died in 840, however, the great empire was weakened by fighting among his three heirs, each of whom wanted the Carolingian throne. In 843, the heirs signed the Treaty of Verdun, dividing the empire into three smaller kingdoms. The first, the West Frankish Kingdom, consisted mainly of the territory that later became France. Another, the East Frankish Kingdom, occupied Germanic lands east of the Rhine River. Between the two lay the aptly named Middle Kingdom (much of which later became Italy). In 870, the leader of the Middle Kingdom died, and the East and West kingdoms divided his territory by signing the Treaty of Mersen.

Gradually, new regional powers emerged from within the East Kingdom, particularly in Bavaria, Franconia, Saxony, Thuringia, and Swabia, the kingdom's five duchies (states ruled by dukes). These states' dukes and nobles wanted to pursue individual and regional interests rather than the aims of their king's central government. Wealthy and influential, the aristocrats were able to do as they wished, and the authority of the East Kingdom monarch and his successors weakened. The pursuit of individual interests over obedience to the central government—known as "particularism"—would guide the course of Germanic politics for most of the next seven centuries.

In 918, the growing strength of aristocrats, repeated enemy invasions, and the death of the last Carolingian king triggered the collapse of the entire Carolingian Empire, both East and West. Later, historians would call the Carolingian period the First Reich (empire). It represented the first in a series of distinct eras in German history.

The Saxons and Salians

After the Carolingian Empire fell, the dukes of Bavaria, Franconia, Saxony, and Swabia elected the duke of Franconia king of Germany, under the title Conrad I. But in 919, they became disenchanted with Conrad's rule and elected a new king from the Saxon tribe—Henry the Fowler, or Henry I. The new king ruled for 17 years; upon his death in 936, power passed to his son, Otto I, also called Otto the Great. Otto accepted the imperial crown and became ruler of both the Germanic Empire and the Holy Roman Empire, affirming his kingdom's ties with the Roman Catholic church and the pope.

With the church's help, Otto and his heirs united the Germanic Empire. They increased their landholdings by seizing territory from the

During the Salian era, nobles built huge castles to illustrate their power.

aristocrats. As a result, regional powers lost influence and the crown gained dominance over them. The Saxon Dynasty also began to expand its claims beyond the empire—to Bohemia and Poland in the east, and to Austria and Italy in the south.

In 1024, the last of the Saxon monarchs died, and the German nobles restored power to the Franconians. They began to elect their kings from among the Salians, a Franconian tribe that came from the northern Rhine region. Under the leadership of the Salian kings Conrad II, Henry III, and Henry IV, the Germanic monarchy continued to expand its territory and to become a major European power. The Salians established a permanent administrative system in which a class of hired public officials served the crown. They also encouraged the emergence of independent merchants, who formed the kingdom's first middle class. The towns of Nuremburg and Frankfurt became centers of cultural arts, craftsmanship, and commerce.

Salian rule was challenged in 1075 by the "Investiture Controversy"— a power struggle between the monarchy and the Roman Catholic church that ultimately led to a 47-year civil war. Regional nobles, who wanted more power, allied themselves with the church, which felt that the Salian kings held too much power. The most prominent nobles, or princes, also competed with one another in acquiring larger amounts of land and forming armies. By the time the war ended in 1122, the princes had gained immense power and wealth, and the Salian monarchy had disintegrated.

In 1138, the first king from the Hohenstaufen Dynasty was elected. Although rival families attempted to seize the throne, the Hohenstaufens held it until 1254. Their most famous king was Frederick I—popularly known as Barbarossa—who took the throne in 1152. He ended conflicts among the various Germanic peoples and expanded the empire's influence to the east and south. A dashing and colorful king, Barbarossa inspired many legends. According to one story, he is still sleeping in a cave in the Kyffhauser Mountains and will one day awaken to lead his people again.

After Barbarossa's death in 1190, his son, Henry VI, took the throne. Although Henry continued his father's policies, the monarchy began to lose its hold on the Germanic states. From the 13th through the 15th centuries, kings from rival territorial powers—most notably the Luxemburg, Wittlesbach, and Hapsburg families—followed one another as leaders of the Germanic Empire. The Hapsburgs secured the throne in 1438 and kept it until 1806. But, although some of them were strong rulers, disunity weakened Germany's central government and slowed its political development.

The Renaissance

Despite territorial conflicts and disunity, the Middle Ages was a period of cultural advancement throughout Germany and the rest of Europe. In the 14th century, the Renaissance—an era of intellectual and artistic progress—began. Art, literature, music, and architecture flourished. Great universities sprang up. Large cities developed, and people flocked to these centers of thought and commerce.

The Renaissance produced great philosophers, among them Martin Luther, a German priest who taught at the University of Wittenberg in eastern Germany. Luther believed that some practices of the Roman Catholic church were corrupt. On October 31, 1517, he nailed 95 arguments he had written against the church to the door of a Wittenberg church. Luther's protest against the church spread rapidly throughout Europe, gaining thousands of supporters. As a result, a new religion emerged—Lutheranism, or Protestantism. It preached simple Christian values and individual faith. This period of religious revolution was known as the Reformation.

Luther's teachings echoed the discontent felt by Germany's peasants. Dominated by princes, they blamed the church and the Holy Roman Empire for their lack of power. The revolutionary spark of Luther's Reformation ignited Germany's peasantry into an uprising in 1524.

Although the princes quickly crushed the revolt, a deeper, more widespread disunity began to grow in Germany. During the Reformation, many

Germans in the south continued to support Catholicism and ties to Rome. By the early 17th century, religious differences deeply divided northern and southern Germany. Roman Catholics, seeking to regain the power they had lost to the Protestants, began the Catholic Counter-Reformation, a movement designed to weaken Protestant influence.

In 1618, the Holy Roman emperor Matthias sought to restore Catholicism to Bohemia, an area of the empire that had become largely Protestant. Bohemia's Protestant nobles revolted, triggering the Thirty Years' War, one of the bitterest battles in history. By the time the bloody war ended in 1648, Germany lay in ruins. Its population had been reduced by almost one-third, many people had fallen into utter poverty, and thousands of towns, villages, and castles had been destroyed.

Luther's arguments against the Catholic church gave birth to Protestantism.

A statue honors Frederick the Great, who made Prussia into a powerful state.

The most significant result of the war, however, was the dissolution of the German Empire. The agreement that ended the war, the Treaty of Westphalia, granted the princes authority to govern their domains independently. Hundreds of sovereignties (independent domains) were carved from the former empire.

The Rise of Prussia

By the beginning of the 18th century, Germany was a fragmented collection of mini-states. One of these mini-states was Brandenburg-Prussia, in northern Germany. The area had suffered greatly during the Thirty Years' War. Immediately after the war, therefore, it formed a huge army to defend itself against its neighboring states.

Brandenburg-Prussia's 200,000-man defensive army quickly turned offensive. By the mid-18th century, Frederick William the Great, king of Prussia, had nearly doubled the size of the kingdom by conquering adjacent regions. Frederick imposed a harsh rule on the conquered territories, but he modernized government and society. By the time he died in 1786, Prussia was one of the most powerful states in Germany, second only to the many allied territories of the long-dominant Hapsburg Dynasty.

Although the wars started by the Prussians severely damaged Germany's economic life, its intellectual life thrived. Classical musicians, including Mozart and Bach, composed breathtaking symphonies, baroque art and architecture flourished, and philosophers such as Immanuel Kant and Johann Wolfgang von Goethe rose to prominence.

A Series of Revolutions

In 1789, a revolution shook neighboring France, and the French monarchy was deposed. France's new leader, a young military officer named Napoleon Bonaparte, immediately launched a series of fierce attacks on other European nations. Swiftly, he conquered much of Germany. Even Prussia's army was no match for his forces. By 1807, Napoleon had seized control of the Prussian capital and other German regions, including Austria. To unite the German empire under his rule, Napoleon created the Confederation of the Rhine—a political alliance between France and the German states near the Rhine River.

In 1813, Prussia rose up and led the other German states to victory against Napoleon in the War of Liberation. In 1815, after Napoleon and his troops met their defeat at Waterloo, leaders of European nations met in a conference called the Congress of Vienna. They dissolved the Confederation of the Rhine and redrew the boundaries of Germany's states to form a new German Confederation. The Congress also reduced the number of German monarchies to 38 and permitted each state to draw up a constitution. It also permitted the nobles of each state to elect a legislative assembly, or parliament. A central assembly in Austria presided over the confederation.

Despite these political changes, the new confederation did not restore peace in Germany. In the mid-1840s, Germany's lower and middle classes demanded political reform. German liberals, led by Karl Marx and Fried-rich Engels, called for a free press, trial by jury, a national militia to replace the old aristocratic army, and a parliament elected by the people. In some cities, violence erupted over these issues. When another revolution took place in France in February 1848, many Germans joined the revolutionary spirit by fighting in the streets of Vienna and Prussian cities.

Some states responded to these uprisings by establishing constitutions that met the revolutionaries' demands. In May 1848, representatives from each German state met in Frankfurt and formed the German National Assembly. They drafted the Declaration of Fundamental Rights, a constitution modeled after those of France and the United States. The assembly proposed to replace the separate state monarchies with a single national monarchy, and it asked the king of Prussia—Frederick William IV—to head the new government. But hopes for a united Germany were dashed when the Prussian king rejected the proposal. The National Assembly dissolved, and quarrels among the revolutionaries, combined with a conservative counterrevolution, further weakened the unification movement. As a result, the two most powerful states, Prussia and Austria, regained their dominance over Germany.

Bismarck and Unification

Prussia's dominance grew under the rule of its powerful prime minister-president Otto von Bismarck, who rose to power in 1848. Bismarck wanted to reunify Germany, but he did not believe that the states could be governed democratically. Instead, he planned to impose Prussian leadership on all the states through military conquest.

From 1864 to 1870, Bismarck launched a series of wars against French, Austrian, and Danish territories in Germany. As a result, he won control of the northern province of Schweslig-Holstein (which had been ruled by the Danes) and the territories of Alsace and Lorraine (formerly under French rule). By 1871, Prussia had annexed two-thirds of all German regions and had emerged as the dominant force in central Europe.

Once he gained these regions, Bismarck continued his plan to reunify them. He proclaimed the Second Reich, forging the first modern German nation. He had the Prussian king William I crowned *kaiser* (emperor), and had himself named chancellor. The new reich installed a parliament, or Reichstag, and adopted a new constitution.

Through aggressive foreign and economic policies, the Second Reich raised Germany to the ranks of a world power. A spirit of national pride and confidence filled the German people. But in 1890, Bismarck, the "Iron Chancellor," stepped down, and the Second Reich began to crumble. His successors lacked his political and diplomatic skills and were unable to stand up to Kaiser William II, who had assumed the throne in 1888. The kaiser recklessly interfered in world affairs, starting conflicts in Russia and France.

In 1914, the kaiser's interventions led to the outbreak of World War I. On June 28, a man from the small Eastern European state of Serbia assassinated Austria's Archduke Ferdinand. The kaiser took Austria's side against Russia and the Serbs; when Russia mobilized its troops on July 31, Germany declared war.

Bismarck unified Germany and made it a world power.

World War I and the Weimar Republic

Germany entered World War I with high hopes. By 1914, it was Europe's largest producer of iron and steel and had a large, well-trained army and a powerful navy. The German people believed their cause was just and were confident that they would quickly emerge victorious. By 1917, German armies had battered Russia to defeat, and in early 1918 they achieved some stunning victories against the Western Allies, which now included the United States.

In the long run, however, the Allies proved too strong for Germany, and in November 1918 the German government surrendered. On November 9, 1918, a new German government called the Weimar Republic was proclaimed. With the monarchial and state governments replaced by Socialist councils, the Weimar Republic represented a compromise between Germany's new Social Democratic party and its old conservative Prussian leadership.

The next year, the republic's leaders signed the Treaty of Versailles, officially ending World War I. The treaty forced Germany to disband its armed forces, give up its overseas colonies, and surrender some of its European territory (including the Rhineland and most of West Prussia). The treaty also required Germany to pay heavy financial reparations.

The treaty upset many Germans and undermined their confidence in the Weimar Republic. It also isolated Germany from its Western European neighbors. Soon, the republic began to disintegrate. It was weakened by continual changes in leadership (during its 14-year lifespan, the Weimar Republic changed governments 20 times). It was also plagued by a series of economic crises, including severe inflation in the early 1920s and total economic collapse during the Great Depression of the early 1930s. Growing dissatisfaction with the Weimar government caused political unrest throughout Germany.

Many Germans blamed the Weimar government for Germany's loss in World War I and for all of its subsequent problems. During the 1920s, many political parties sprang up to appeal to these disgruntled German

Germany's cities thrived before World War I, but after the war the economy crumbled.

nationalists. One of these was the fledgling National Socialist, or Nazi, party. The Nazis claimed that Socialists, Communists, and Jews controlled the Weimar government and were therefore responsible for Germany's problems. In 1923, they attempted to overthrow the Weimar government.

The Nazi rebellion failed, and many Nazi leaders were imprisoned. One of them was Adolf Hitler, a former corporal in the German army.

Hitler spent nine months in jail. At the time he was released, the Nazi party held little influence in German politics. But as dissatisfaction with the Weimar government increased, so did support for the Nazis. Many Germans welcomed the Nazis' promises of economic revitalization and their demand for revision of the Treaty of Versailles. Over the next ten years, the Nazis continued to win support. And as their power grew, so did Adolf Hilter's. By the early 1930s, Hitler was leading the party. In 1933, supported by the right-wing Nationalist party and military forces, Hitler and the Nazis seized control of the government and set up a military dictatorship known as the Third Reich.

The Nazi Regime

Hitler's government at first seemed promising. To the overwhelming approval of the German people, the Nazis rebuilt Germany's industrial and military strength. But beneath the surface, Hitler's regime was brutal and racist. Nazi doctrine preached racial purity and anti-Semitism (hatred of Jews). Hitler and his ministers told the public that Germanic peoples were the "master race" and that all others should be purged from society. People designated as enemies of the party were exiled or executed. Millions of German Jews, who had formed a prosperous and influential minority, were sent to concentration camps, where the Nazis tortured and murdered them.

Meanwhile, the Nazis were secretly mobilizing for war. In 1939, they invaded neighboring Poland, provoking Poland's allies, Great Britain and France, to declare war. Soon, other nations became embroiled in the conflict, which rapidly became World War II. The Axis powers (Germany, Italy, Hungary, Romania, and Bulgaria) fought against the Allies (Great Britain, France, the Soviet Union, and the United States) for control of Europe.

At first, the war went well for Germany. At the height of their power, the Germans conquered Poland, Denmark, Norway, Belgium, Luxembourg, the Netherlands, and France. Their battlefield strategy, called

(continued on page 49)

SCENES OF
EAST
GERMANY

➤ *During the 1930s, posters such as this one rallied Germans against communism.*

Deutschlands Sieg
EUROPAS FREIHEIT

∀ *Humboldt University is one of many East German colleges.*

▲ Collective farms provide 90 percent of the nation's food. This farm raises sheep.

▲ Dresden, destroyed during World War II, has been rebuilt.

➤ *This statue commemorates Goethe and Schiller, two great masters of German literature.*

◄ *A billowing smokestack towers over Leipzig, an industrial city in southern East Germany.*

◄ *A poster depicts Karl Marx, the creator of East Germany's Communist system.*

Y *East Berlin, the nation's cultural hub, is home to the Pergamon Museum.*

A toy store window displays the latest dolls and games.

➤ This stone mosaic of a lion decorates an interior wall of the Pergamon Museum.

◄ The serene courtyard of Castle Church in Wittenburg is a popular tourist spot.

➤ *Some old churches feature ornate pulpits.*

➤ *Impressive architecture highlights the city of Erfurt.*

◄ *An ice cream parlor always attracts a hungry crowd.*

⌄ *Allied troops guard "Checkpoint Charlie," on the border between West and East Berlin.*

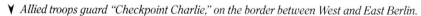

During World War II, the Nazis sent captured Allied soldiers to prisoner-of-war camps.

(Continued from page 40)

krieg (lightning war), pounded the opposition with the quick, coordinated use of tanks, planes, and infantry. Once they conquered an area, they imprisoned thousands of civilians and soldiers in gruesome concentration camps.

In 1943, however, Germany's fortunes turned. The Soviets defeated the Germans at Stalingrad in the Soviet Union and forced them into a long, slow retreat. At about the same time, the Allies gained control of North Africa and forced Germany's partner, Italy, to withdraw from the war. In 1944, the United States and Great Britain attacked the Germans at Normandy in France and drove them back to Germany.

By early 1945, the Soviets had driven the Germans out of the Balkan Mountains in Eastern Europe and the war was lost. On April 30, 1945, Adolf Hilter killed himself; Germany surrendered one week later. The Third Reich had ended, and Germany would never be the same.

Air raids destroyed many German cities during World War II. In this famous photograph, a statue peers out over Dresden, which was reduced to ruins by Allied bombs.

The Birth of East Germany

At the end of World War II, Germany lay in ruins. Cities had been reduced to rubble, and the economy had been destroyed. In 1945, the victorious Allies—Britain, France, the United States, and the Soviet Union—met at conferences at Yalta in the Soviet Union and Potsdam in Germany to determine Germany's future. They divided Germany and its capital city, Berlin, into four occupied zones, each supervised by one of the Allies.

Originally, the Allies planned to reunite Germany's four zones. But they could not agree on the best type of government for the country. France, Britain, and the United States wanted a democratic government for Germany; the Soviet Union envisioned a Communist state. As disagreement intensified, the opposing powers strengthened their influence in their zones. In 1948, the Soviets blockaded Berlin in an attempt to seize control of the city.

The Soviets lifted their blockade in 1949. But plans for reuniting Germany had changed drastically. On May 23, 1949, Britain, France, and the United States combined their zones to form a new, independent country—the Federal Republic of Germany, or West Germany. In October of that same year, the Soviet-occupied zone also became a separate nation—the German Democratic Republic (GDR), or East Germany. Berlin was divided into two cities, and East Berlin became the capital of the GDR. And although it lay deep within East Germany, West Berlin became part of West Germany.

The Soviets immediately began putting their stamp on East Germany. They transferred lands east of the Oder and Neisse rivers to Poland. They confiscated machinery, livestock, and transportation and communications equipment and sent it to the Soviet Union. And to ensure their influence on the new nation, they quickly began to restructure East Germany in their own Communist image. One-third of the country's farmland, previously owned by about 3,000 landlords, was divided among more than 500,000 farmworkers. All large industrial operations became government property. Nazi elements were eliminated from the schools, courts, and police departments, and those institutions were redesigned within a Socialist framework. During this process, many East Germans lost their homes and jobs and were reduced to poverty.

The Soviets allowed the East Germans to form political parties, but they carefully monitored all political activity. In April 1946, they arranged for the Communist and Social Democratic parties to merge into the Social-

During the Soviet blockade, the United States sent food supplies to Berlin.

ist Unity party (SED). The new party soon dominated East German politics.

In May 1949, a people's congress of 1,525 elected members adopted a new constitution for the GDR and elected Wilhelm Pieck as its president. It also created the post of secretary-general (later called first secretary) of the SED, the most powerful position in the government. In 1950, Soviet-trained Walter Ulbricht became secretary-general.

The SED Government

In 1951, the SED congress unveiled a five-year plan for the GDR's economy. The plan, which closely resembled Soviet economic strategies, called for increased production by workers. Many East Germans resented the plan, and in June 1953, public anger over job pressures, food shortages, and overall "Sovietization" of GDR affairs erupted in strikes and rioting. As a result, the Soviets gradually yielded direct control of the nation to the East Germans.

Despite this change, many East Germans continued to disapprove of government policies. Between 1945 and 1961, more than 3.5 million East Germans left their country for Western nations. Most of these defectors were young and well educated, and many fled to neighboring West Germany. The most common escape route was through West Berlin.

This steady flight of citizens worried GDR officials, and in 1961 they constructed a blockade between East and West Berlin. Known as the Berlin Wall, the 15-foot- (5-meter-) high barricade stretches for 99.5 miles (160 kilometers) between East and West Berlin. The GDR installed border patrols, machine gun towers, guard dogs, tank traps, trip mines, alarms, television monitors, and listening devices to prevent anyone from crossing the wall into West Berlin. Although a few people dared to challenge the wall, the steady flow of young people out of East Germany was reduced to a trickle.

This reduction in emigration forced many young, educated East Germans into the work force. Combined with new economic planning, this

The Soviets took farmland away from landlords and divided it among farm workers.

helped the GDR to make rapid economic progress. In 1963, the government introduced the New Economic System, which allowed people at lower organizational levels of industry to make more decisions about productivity. The system stressed managerial and technical training and rewarded excellent job performance. The new strategies succeeded. The GDR's industrial output and its standard of living improved dramatically.

In the late 1960s, however, economic growth slowed. To speed it up again, the government decided to replace top SED officials. In 1971, Walter Ulbricht was removed from the first secretary's job and replaced by Erich Honecker.

Honecker's economic program for the 1970s called for a better quality of life for workers. Wages, pensions, and child care improved. Housing remained inexpensive and became more readily available. Television sets, automobiles, and other consumer goods became more available and affordable.

Honecker supported détente (a loosening of tensions between nations) with the West. Under his leadership, East Germany signed the Four Powers Agreement on Berlin in September 1971. It allowed easier travel and commerce between East Germany and Western countries. In December 1972, the Honecker government also signed the Basic Treaty with West Germany, in which the two Germanies pledged to respect one another's borders.

Nevertheless, Honecker's government also strengthened its ties to the Soviet Union. In 1974, the East German constitution was amended to make the strong bonds between the two nations official. As a result, East Germany became more firmly entrenched in the Communist bloc and strengthened its ties with the other European Communist-bloc nations: Hungary, Czechoslovakia, Poland, and Bulgaria.

The early 1980s brought renewed tensions to the East-West relationship, and Honecker's government began to cut back on relations with its Western neighbors. In 1981, West German Chancellor Helmut Schmidt traveled to the GDR to speak with Honecker, but two years later, Honecker canceled a planned visit to West Germany after a violent border incident in which a North Atlantic Treaty Organization (NATO) border guard was killed. The situation worsened in late 1983 after the United States moved nuclear missiles into West Germany. The Soviets responded by installing more of their missiles in East Germany.

More recently, however, relations between East Germany and the West have improved. In 1984, 40,000 East German citizens—mostly older people—were allowed to emigrate to the West. In 1985, Honecker met with West German Chancellor Helmut Kohl at the funeral of Soviet Premier Konstantin Chernenko in Moscow. Furthermore, Soviet leader Mikhail Gorbachev seems to be encouraging better relations between East Germany and West Germany.

But East-West tensions continue. Because East Germany is so closely allied with the Soviet Union and because West Germany and other Western nations follow the United States's lead, any tension between the superpowers weakens relations between East Germany and the West.

Because of World War II and its effects, women make up almost half of East Germany's labor force and more than half of its population.

The People of the GDR

About 16,900,000 people live in the German Democratic Republic. A full 99 percent of them are descended from the ancient Teutonic tribes that occupied Germany thousands of years ago. There are also about 100,000 Sorbs (a German-Slavic people with a unique language and culture dating from the 6th century) and about 3,500 Jews.

In the 20th century, East Germany's population has been affected by two factors: World War II and postwar emigration. So many East German men were killed in the war that, even today, women greatly outnumber men. The loss of so many men also affected East Germany's marriage and birth rates—both drastically declined in the postwar years. And thousands of young men left the country between 1949 and 1961, decreasing the marriage and birth rates still further. As a result, nearly one-fifth of the population is of retirement age, and older women outnumber older men by almost two-to-one. Women make up almost 50 percent of the labor force, and 70 percent of women between the ages of 15 and 59 work for a living.

Most East Germans live and work in the heavily industrialized cities. Manufacturing employs about 40 percent of the total work force. About 11 percent of East Germans work in agriculture, and about 3 percent form the "technical intelligentsia"—planners, scientists, engineers, and high-level bureaucrats. Another 1 percent make up the political elite—citizens who hold important positions in the dominant Socialist Unity party, or SED.

Job opportunities are varied and plentiful, and incomes are comfortable. East Germans have one of the highest standards of living in Eastern Europe. The average income for workers has tripled since 1950. Today, most workers earn about 1,100 GDR-marks (about U.S. $407) per month. But while income has increased, prices have not. The government ensures that consumer expenses remain the same. Housing costs about $37 per month, and food is also inexpensive. The country produces most of its staples, such as meat, butter, eggs, and milk, so prices for these foods are low. An East German can buy a quart (approximately a liter) of milk for the equivalent of about U.S. 30 cents.

Outings to restaurants, concerts, and sporting events are much cheaper than in most Western countries. Public transportation costs are also minimal: second-class rail fare for a 30-mile (48-kilometer) trip costs

The government lets people attend churches, including the Church of Peace in Potsdam.

less than U.S. $1.50, and trolley fares are equivalent to about U.S. 10 cents. Automobile prices start at about 10,000 GDR-marks (U.S. $3,704).

Some items are not cheaper than in the West, however. The prices of many consumer goods are higher than prices in the United States or Western European countries. For example, a refrigerator costs about 1,100 GDR-marks, or one month's salary for most East Germans. A color television set costs even more—about 5,000 GDR-marks (U.S. $1,852). But despite the high prices, more and more East Germans are purchasing these luxury items.

The Family

East Germans believe that the family is the most important unit in society. To overcome the downward population trend, the government encourages large families by offering incentives such as free child care and paid maternity leaves.

Traditionally, Germany was a strongly patriarchal society, meaning that men held unquestioned authority over their households. But today, East German law states that women are completely equal to their husbands and that parents hold joint responsibility for raising and educating their children. Furthermore, a married couple can choose either the wife's or the husband's last name as the family name. The legal marriage age for both men and women is 18.

An average couple earns a joint income of about 1,750 GDR-marks (about U.S. $650) a month. Government funds pay for education, medical and social care, and sometimes even vacations. Most families live in rented apartments and pay about 100 GDR-marks (U.S. $37) a month in rent.

Although the government once discouraged church membership, organized religion is permitted today in the GDR. About 50 percent of the population is Protestant. Most East German Protestants adhere to Lutheranism, the national church started by Martin Luther. About 8 percent of the people are Catholic, and less than 1 percent follow other faiths, such as Judaism.

Historic buildings such as the Royal Opera House recall a rich cultural heritage.

Over the years, the government has attempted to replace religious rites with new social or political ceremonies. The most significant of these new rituals is the *Jugendweihe*, which marks the entry of a youth into adulthood. It usually occurs on a child's 14th birthday (around the same age as the Christian confirmation or the Jewish bar mitzvah). Before the Jugendweihe, the youth is instructed in political and social philosophy. During the ceremony, he or she vows loyalty to the state.

A Rich Cultural Heritage

The East Germans have a rich cultural heritage that spans thousands of years. They are proud of their cultural accomplishments and are committed to preserving them. National celebrations honor the birthdays of renowned German classical music composers, such as Handel and Bach. East German theater companies often present the plays of legendary German writers, such as Friedrich Schiller and Johann von Goethe.

The government has helped to preserve East Germany's culture. For example, it recently restored the Schauspielhaus, an impressive building in East Berlin that was badly damaged in World War II. Rebuilt in time for the GDR's 35th anniversary celebration in October 1984, the Schauspielhaus now serves as a permanent home for the Berlin Symphony Orchestra and for the city's Singakademie, or Choral Society.

Cultural heritage is also celebrated at the Workers Festival, a three-day spectacle of music and dance held every two years in a different East German city. At a recent festival in Gera, a city in the southwest, participants dressed in traditional costumes, performed folk songs and dances, and shared old tribal legends. They also revived the Bird Shoot, a contest that dates back to the 16th century. Bird Shoot contestants fire at wooden birds perched on a rod, and the best marksman wins a crown.

Contemporary Culture

East Germany's government believes in balancing contemporary culture with the SED's beliefs and goals. State-sponsored organizations promote and support most writers, musicians, dancers, painters, filmmakers, pho-

The government has preserved examples of German architecture, such as this retreat.

tographers, and other artists. These organizations fund study grants, educational trips, and contracts to help young artists' careers. The government ensures incomes for artists of whose work it approves.

Many great artists have emerged from the GDR. Among them are novelists Hermann Kant, Arnold Zweig, and Christa Wolf and the late poet-playwright Bertolt Brecht. Noted East German filmmakers include Lothar Warneke, Herman Zschoche, and the late Konrad Wolf.

East German art-lovers can enjoy their country's 81 state-supported orchestras, 98 music schools, 48 theater companies, 40 ballet ensembles, and more than 600 museums and galleries. In addition, the government sponsors amateur involvement in the arts as well. The main showcase for amateur activities is the Workers Festival.

All this government interest in the arts carries a price, however. Art is strictly censored. Artists and writers are forbidden to criticize the government in any way, and they are discouraged from creating artworks that cannot be appreciated by the mass public. As a result, many artists and writers are among those East Germans who feel the government is too repressive.

The East German identity is perhaps most strongly expressed in the German language. One of the world's most widely spoken languages, German spans the East-West border. Although the GDR government has tried to develop a distinctly East German language, it has not been very successful. The easing of travel restrictions between East Germany and West Germany has brought greater contact between citizens of the two nations, discouraging the development of language differences. Perhaps most important, television and radio broadcasts from both countries use the shared German language and are received on either side of the border.

The Sporting Life

Sports are a prominent form of cultural expression in East Germany. One citizen in five is athletically active. Communities throughout the country have swimming pools, soccer and volleyball fields, gymnasiums, and bowl-

East German schools emphasize sports. These students celebrate a handball victory.

ing alleys. Hiking and jogging routes wind through the cities and countryside.

Sport is an important subject in East German schools. Athletically gifted children meet at the National Spartakiad Games, held every two years at a different location. Thousands of older athletes take part in the Sports and Gymnastic Festival, held every four years in Leipzig.

Its dedication to athletic excellence has placed East Germany among the top three medal-winning countries at every Olympic Games since 1968. At the 1984 Winter Olympics, East German athletes won nine gold, nine silver, and six bronze medals. Speed skaters Karin Enke and Andrea Schone, figure skater Katerina Witt, ski jumper Jens Weissflog, and bobsled driver Wolfgang Hoppe were among the high achievers on the 1984 team. Because the GDR blends sports training with solid academic and vocational instruction, many of its top athletes become skilled workers, teachers, engineers, and doctors after their careers of athletic competition are over.

Most East Germans live in the nation's cities, many of which have existed for centuries. Dresden, above, has been a cultural center for hundreds of years.

A Wealth of Great Cities

Almost three-quarters of East Germany's people live in its major cities, most of which are clustered in the southern third of the country. Cities are the country's economic and cultural centers. Many of them are centuries old, yet they combine tradition with modern conveniences and ways of life. Because the cities are so densely populated, the government is trying to improve urban environments for residents and workers.

The largest city in East Germany is Berlin, located 40 miles (64 kilometers) from the Polish border and about 100 miles (161 kilometers) from the West German border. Founded in the 13th century, Berlin was the greatest city in pre-World War II Germany. By the 1920s, it had become the cultural capital of all of central Europe. Today, Berlin is divided into two cities, East and West Berlin, which are separated by the menacing steel and concrete of the Berlin Wall.

East Berlin has a population of 1.2 million, and covers 165 square miles (429 square kilometers)—about half the area of the old Berlin. It serves as the nation's capital. The headquarters of the East German government and the embassies and missions of more than 130 countries are located there.

The city is also the largest industrial center in the GDR. It is especially important for its electronics and mechanical engineering work. Canals link it with the Oder and Elbe rivers, enabling the transport of goods by water. Internationally important railroads, highways, and air routes also intersect at East Berlin.

Over the past few decades, government-supervised reconstruction has revitalized East Berlin's commercial and residential areas, which were reduced to rubble in World War II. Now, people shop in its well-stocked supermarkets, travel on its first-class subway system, and attend its fine schools.

The city's cultural attractions include many museums, most notably the Pergamon Museum and the Bode Museum. Its famous theaters and operahouses include the Deutsches Theater, the Berliner Ensemble, and the State Opera House, which was rebuilt twice—first after a fire in 1934,

This castle escaped the bombs that destroyed much of Berlin during the war.

and again after World War II. East Berlin's many technical schools and colleges include Humboldt University, which was badly damaged in World War II but rebuilt soon afterward.

Because East Berlin is such an old city, it reflects centuries of architectural change. The Marien Church, originally built in the 14th century, stands near the Alexanderplatz, the city's main square. Just a short distance from the church looms the 1,197-foot- (359-meter-) high Television Tower, which opened in 1969. Another architectural marvel is the Museum of German History, a masterpiece of 17th-century baroque style marked by intricate ornamental figures.

The ultramodern East German parliament building stands at one end of the tree-lined Unter den Linden, once Berlin's main thoroughfare. At the other end is the Brandenburg Gate, one of East Berlin's most famous landmarks. Completed in 1791, it was designed as a "gate of peace." However, it was repeatedly battered by war and revolution. Now fully restored, it stands close to the Berlin Wall as a reminder of Berlin's troubled and violent past. Just east of the gate is the heavily guarded point of entry through the Berlin Wall that leads into West Berlin. To the people of Western nations, it is known as "Checkpoint Charlie."

Leipzig

With a population of about 550,000, Leipzig is the GDR's second largest city. Located in the south central region, the 800-year-old city has developed into an international cultural and trading center.

Leipzig is a vital industrial city. It leads the country in fur production and manufactures mining ores, chemicals, farm machinery, and printing presses. Twice a year, Leipzig hosts international trade shows where exhibitors display goods ranging from minicomputers and revolving cranes to musical instruments and running shoes.

The city's cultural life centers around the high-rise buildings of Karl Marx University, where thousands of foreign students attend German-language classes at the Herder Institute. The city is home to many book

Western tourists may now explore East Germany's ancient wonders, such as this old arched gate near the city of Templin in the northeastern GDR.

and sheet music publishers and to the Deutsches Bucherei, a library that has collected German-language literature for more than 60 years. The city also hosts the renowned Leipzig Book Fair, which attracts publishers from around the world.

On Market Square, the 16th-century Altes Rathaus (Old Town Hall) reflects the city's first period of commercial prosperity. Near the square is St. Thomas Church, where the great composer Johann Sebastian Bach lived and worked. Leipzig's musical traditions are carried on by the St. Thomas Boys' Choir, the Gewandhaus Orchestra, and the College of Music. The city also features 18 museums and 5 municipal theaters.

Dresden

Like many other cities in the GDR, Dresden, a city of 520,000 in the country's southeastern sector, has been a cultural center for centuries.

The Kreuzchor, or Church of the Cross Choir, has existed since the Middle Ages. The 19th-century composer Richard Wagner wrote several famous operas while living in Dresden, and nine of composer Richard Strauss's operas opened there during the first half of the 20th century. The city has two symphony orchestras, four theater companies, and many fine art galleries.

Dresden is also an industrial city, East Germany's center for vehicle manufacturing, microelectronics, light industry, and food processing.

Considered a model city when this photo was taken in 1906, Dresden is now an industrial center.

Some of its products include electric motors, X-ray equipment, and cameras. More than 13,000 students attend the city's University of Technology. Dresden's German Hygiene Museum and the nuclear research center at nearby Rossendorf are among the GDR's leading scientific institutes.

Dresden was leveled in 1945 during one of World War II's fiercest bombing raids. However, many of the historic buildings have been carefully reconstructed. Some of Germany's most beautiful buildings are located in the city. The Zwinger, a festival square enclosed by art galleries and other buildings, was built in the early 18th century and is the most celebrated piece of German baroque architecture. The Opera House was built between 1871 and 1878 in the Italian Renaissance style, reflecting ancient Greek and Roman architecture. The Institute and Museum of Civic History is housed in an 18th-century structure that combines late baroque with classical Greek and Roman features.

Other Cities

Karl Marx City, with about 320,000 inhabitants, lies in the south central uplands region. Founded in the 12th century, it was known as Chemnitz until 1953, when its name was changed to commemorate the Communist

The Old Gateway leads to Potsdam, a historic city only a few miles west of Berlin.

philosopher. Once a maze of narrow and crooked streets, the city has been rebuilt into a modern center. Its industries produce automobiles, motorcycles, and office machinery. It is also a popular recreational area because of its location in the Ore Mountains.

Another important city is Magdeburg, with a population of 290,000. Located on the Elbe River in the west central region, the city boasts the largest inland harbor, as well as the most farmland, in the entire country. In its 1,000-year history, Magdeburg has experienced both prosperity and near destruction. Today, its restored cathedral overlooks many blocks of modern apartment buildings.

Rostock is a Baltic seaport with a population of 235,000, making it the largest town in the coastal region. Since World War II, it has become a major center for shipbuilding and cargo transport. Its shipbuilding industry constructs ships for the GDR's merchant fleet as well as for sale to other countries.

Halle, in the southwest, is the chief city of the GDR's most industrially productive county. Halle specializes in mechanical engineering and manufacturing-plant construction, and most of the city's 232,000 residents are employed in these industries. The city's Marktkirche (Marketplace Church) was one of Martin Luther's favorite preaching places. Composer Georg Friedrich Handel was born in Halle in 1685.

To the southwest of Halle is Erfurt, a city of 212,000 people. Erfurt is best known for its electrical engineering industry and its annual international flower show.

Other large East German cities include Schwerin in the north, Zwickau in the south, and Potsdam in the eastern central region, each of which has a population of about 125,000. Southern industrial towns, such as Gera and Gena, have populations of slightly more than 100,000 each.

The Socialist Unity party (SED) runs East Germany's government from East Berlin, where armed soldiers guard government buildings.

Government and Economy

The German Democratic Republic is a Communist nation, and its highly centralized system of government is modeled on the Soviet Union's. Although its first constitution provided for widespread political participation, the Socialist Union party (SED) has always dominated the East German government. In 1968, a new constitution officially established the SED as the country's leading political force.

Today, the SED, which the government calls the "party of the working class," still controls all branches and levels of East Germany's government. Its chief official, the first secretary, is also the country's head of state. Presently, Erich Honecker holds these positions. Under Honecker's authority, national policy is determined by the SED Politburo, the party's principal executive and decision-making committee. The Politburo's 18 members are elected by the Central Committee, an executive body that administers the Politburo's decisions through a network of councils and parliaments. The most powerful parliament is the Volkskammer (People's Chamber), a popularly elected legislative body consisting of 500 representatives and a president. Its delegates, elected to five-year terms, form committees to regulate industry, education, defense, and other foreign and domestic matters. Under the law, five political parties and four mass organizations (large civic and trade associations) are represented in the People's Chamber. The 2.2 million-member SED holds 127 of the chamber's seats.

The SED carefully screens and selects members. A person's character, residence, and occupation are all taken into account when determining whether he or she can become a party member. Because acceptance is regarded as an honor, SED members are the elite class in East Germany. They hold all important positions in government, industry, and the armed forces.

Other state-authorized political parties also exist. The Christian Democratic union, the Democratic Farmers party, the Liberal Democratic party, and the National Democratic party are East Germany's most important minority parties, with about 100,000 members each. They all accept the policies issued by the SED, and although each party is allotted a fixed number of seats in the People's Chamber, the SED always holds the greatest number of seats. Nevertheless, minority parties are active in the GDR's political system. They help to involve East Germany's middle classes in the government process. They also help establish diplomatic ties with political groups in other countries.

A group of 25 People's Chamber members make up the Staatsrat (Council of State), one of two executive-level councils. The council approves or nullifies treaties and works with the National Security Council on matters of defense and security. It also appoints diplomats, monitors elections, and supervises the activities of the Supreme Court and the general prosecutor. The head of state chairs the council.

The other executive council is the 44-member Council of Ministers, or cabinet. All political parties are represented in this council, which executes the GDR's political, economic, cultural, and social policies. Ministers serve five-year terms. The cabinet's chairman also serves as the GDR's prime minister. (After the head of state, the prime minister and the People's Chamber president are the most powerful officials in the SED hierarchy.)

National policies filter down through 15 Bezirkes, or regional districts, each of which has its own parliament. Counties, districts, towns, boroughs, and villages have similar assemblies. However, these councils act only to administer the decisions made by the national government.

East Germany has never held competitive elections. Legislative delegates and members of executive councils are named by the National Front, an SED-dominated group that coordinates political parties and mass organizations. Voters then merely endorse the list of candidates compiled by the National Front.

Mass Organizations

Mass organizations, large social and political clubs, were formed specifically to involve workers in the political process. The largest mass organization is the Free German Trade Union Federation (FDGB). About 96 percent of the country's workers belong to this organization, which holds the second largest number of seats in the People's Chamber.

Like minority political parties, mass organizations accept SED authority. In fact, many FDGB deputies are also SED members. Other SED-

The government continues to rebuild war-damaged buildings in East Berlin.

directed mass organizations include the Free German Youth, which is modeled after the SED and includes many students and soldiers; the Democratic Women's Federation, which helps ensure equal rights for women; and the Cultural League of the GDR, which promotes arts and leisure activities approved by the SED.

The Judicial System

The Supreme Court is the GDR's highest judicial body. Its members are selected by the People's Chamber and the Council of State. Below the Supreme Court is a statewide system of lower courts that handle civil, labor, criminal, and family disputes. Lower court judges are nominated by mass organizations and political parties and are elected by community members during public meetings.

The justice system also includes the German People's Police, which was established in 1946 under Soviet supervision. Citizens are encouraged to play an active role in helping the police maintain order and security. As a result, volunteer fire brigades, road safety committees, and other civic-minded groups abound in the GDR.

Armed Forces and Defense

The East German armed forces, collectively called the National People's Army, include 167,000 ground troops and about 73,000 border soldiers. About 16,000 East Germans serve in the navy, and about 38,000 in the air force. Another 400,000 citizens serve in militias organized at factories and other workplaces. However, most of these soldiers are not full-time military personnel.

As of 1980, roughly half of the members of the armed forces had been drafted. GDR law requires 18 months of military service for all males between the ages of 18 and 26. In addition, all males up to the age of 50 are legally liable for additional service. In times of national crisis, women between the ages of 18 and 50 may be drafted to serve in the medical or supply services.

The GDR has a mutual-defense treaty with the Soviet Union and is a member of the Warsaw Pact (a military alliance of Eastern European states). In 1968, army units from the GDR, the Soviet Union, and three other Warsaw Pact countries invaded Czechoslovakia in order to over-throw the liberal Czech government of President Alexander Dubček. The GDR has also exerted its military strength in developing third-world countries, particularly those in Africa and Asia.

Health and Social Welfare

East Germans benefit from many state-funded health care and social welfare programs. Most medical treatment is paid for by the government, and doctors, nurses, and other medical personnel receive government paychecks. For insured people and their nonworking dependents, all medical and dental service is free. Insurance costs are deducted from paychecks and amount to about 10 percent of most people's wages.

Workers are entitled to up to six weeks' sick leave at 90 percent of their regular pay. Those who are injured on the job receive full pay for lost time, and permanently disabled people receive pensions.

Women may retire from work at age 60 and men at age 65. After retirement, all workers are entitled to government pensions. However, although the government recently increased pensions by 12 percent, pen-

The government funds most hospital treatment and physician training programs.

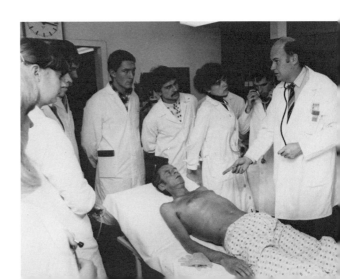

sioners still receive considerably less than the average worker. To help these low-income elderly people, a volunteer group called "Volksolidarrat" (People's Solidarity) provides meals and household help. The government partially pays nursing home costs.

Some government programs help young families. For example, working women are entitled to paid maternity leaves of up to 26 months (depending on the number of children they already have). To further assist working mothers, the state has recently expanded its system of day nurseries. About 70 percent of children up to the age of three can now be looked after while their parents work. Facilities for the physically or mentally handicapped are also increasing, and the government is trying to place handicapped people in workshops and special programs.

Education

The GDR's state-run educational system is free, and there are no private schools. Standardized education for many East German children begins at an early age. Infants and children up to three years of age attend day-care centers and nursery schools, where games and other activities enforce the values and goals of East German society. Almost 70 percent of children aged three to six attend kindergarten. Most kindergartners also attend after-school programs for homework or sports.

When they reach age six, children enter a ten-year general studies program. Attendance in the program is mandatory. In grades four through six, pupils are introduced to the sciences and begin to learn the Russian language. They also study German literature, art, history, and geography and participate in sports. Teachers stress the connection between education and work and the importance of work in a Socialist society.

In grades seven through ten, students receive vocational training at a manufacturing plant or on a farm. During these years, they learn other languages—including English or French—but spend most of their time studying science and technology. Most East German students also belong to political youth organizations such as the Free German Youth. These groups coordinate social events and other activities in the schools and provide labor assistance on government projects.

After the ten-year program, pupils may stay in school for two years of college preparatory work or pursue two more years of vocational training. Some students enter a three-year program that combines advanced scholastic courses with vocational training.

College admission is based on an entrance examination and membership status in a political youth organization. Like all other education in East Germany, college is free. In 1984, 298,000 students were studying at the GDR's colleges, universities, and engineering and technical schools. Technical education lasts three years, and university study ranges from four to five years.

The state tells colleges which courses to offer. Because the government emphasizes advanced technology, most students study subjects such as engineering, economics, medicine, dentistry, and education. About 60 percent of the students at technical schools study full-time. The rest are workers taking night classes or correspondence courses. The government encourages workers to enroll in these adult education programs to better their chances for job promotions. The GDR thinks it is important to tailor education to economic goals. This has helped East Germany to become one of the world's stablest and most advanced economic powers.

An Industrialized Economy

World War II destroyed many industries in both western and eastern Germany. The young GDR suffered additional setbacks because its new boundaries isolated it from important mineral resources in the west. Furthermore, the Soviet Union confiscated much of the GDR's cargo transportation equipment, and war casualties and emigration to West Germany drastically reduced the labor force.

Today, East Germany still lacks mineral and labor resources. Nevertheless, it has developed into one of the most advanced and industrialized economies in the world. Industry accounts for about 70 percent of the national income and employs more than 40 percent of the work force. More than 98 percent of the GDR's industry and agriculture is state-owned. This includes industrial plants, construction firms, and agricultural cooperatives or collectives, where farmers work together on state-owned tracts. There are a few privately owned businesses in East Germany, mostly small farms or shops, but they are the exception.

The GDR's economic success is the result of the SED's constant determination to update its technology, educate its work force, and develop new products. Updating technology sometimes means introducing automation—replacing human workers with machines. The GDR's most productive industries—machinery, chemicals, microelectronics, and consumer goods—are becoming more automated as technology improves. Automation also helps compensate for the country's relatively small labor force.

The government is dedicated to further increasing the country's productivity, and in the early 1980s, it launched an energy conservation program to boost industrial output. In 1984 alone, the GDR mined 296 million tons (329 million metric tons) of crude lignite, met 12 percent of industry's raw material demand through the use of recycled materials, and reduced consumption of fuels, feedstocks for farm animals, and other materials.

As part of the energy conservation program, chemical manufacturing plants use the country's own mineral resources—lignite, potash, and rock salt—efficiently. Vast quantities of these minerals are mined in the uplands and in the Borderland, the area between the uplands and the lowlands. (Other minerals—iron ore, bismuth, cobalt, uranium, and copper—must be imported to supplement existing deposits.) To broaden production, chemical industries are developing plastics and man-made fibers.

Mechanical engineering accounts for more than 20 percent of the country's manufacturing output. It includes production of heavy machinery and motor vehicles. In the 1980s, new types of machines went into production, including computerized offset printing presses and oil-

East German farms provide 90 percent of the food sold in stores such as this one.

extracting machinery. East Germany's microelectronics industry also continues to increase its output and introduce new products. The GDR is one of the few countries in the world that develops and produces microelectronic equipment for use in robots and other automated machinery.

The GDR's output of consumer goods—for use at home and abroad—also continues to grow. In the mid-1980s, newly developed products accounted for more than 20 percent of the industry's output. Some newer products include color televisions, gas heaters, radio cassette recorders, and fashion wear.

The government's plans for increased productivity span industrial manufacturing as well as agriculture. As a result of automation, agriculture now employs only 9 percent of the East German work force, yet it supplies the country with 90 percent of its food. Farmers grow wheat and other grains, fruits, sugar beets, and a variety of vegetables. In 1984, crop yields reached an all-time high—the grain harvest alone reached a record 12 million tons (13 million metric tons). Domestic fodder (animal food) production also increased, and livestock herd levels remained high enough to meet domestic needs.

Most farmers work in large cooperatives, pooling their time and energy to increase production. About 90 percent of farmers complete state-directed agricultural training programs, and about half pass through the state's ten-year general education program.

Foreign Trade

The GDR's economic health depends on foreign trade as well as domestic production. Because the country imports so much fuel and technology, it must sell many goods to other countries to offset the cost of imports. East Germany advances its foreign trade strategies through its membership in the Council of Mutual Economic Assistance, an organization formed to strengthen trade partnerships among Communist countries around the world. About 70 percent of the GDR's trading is with the Soviet Union and the other Communist countries in Eastern Europe—Poland, Hungary, Czechoslovakia, and Bulgaria. About 20 percent of its foreign trade is conducted with capitalist countries, and 5 percent with developing nations of the Third World.

The Soviet Union supplies East Germany with large quantities of steel and natural gas and with about 80 percent of its oil. Gas and oil are brought in through a network of underground pipelines. One oil pipeline extends to a port on the Oder River and then runs 745 miles (1,200 kilometers) to the port of Rostock. A recently completed natural gas pipeline, built with the help of 5,100 members of the Free German Youth, stretches from Siberia to East Germany. In return for fuel imports, the GDR sends chemical equipment, computers, industrial machinery, clothing, and furniture to the Soviet Union.

Some of the GDR's trading partners among the third-world nations, such as Algeria and Iraq, help East Germany meet its crude oil requirements. But the Soviet Union remains the GDR's main supplier of crude oil. Although they recently started charging East Germany more for oil shipments, the Soviets' prices are still cheaper than those of third-world nations.

Other Communist-bloc states provide the GDR with large quantities of raw materials; for example, the GDR gets much of its hard coal from Poland. In return, the other Communist states receive microelectronic technology from the GDR.

Among non-Communist industrialized states, the GDR's biggest trading partner is West Germany. In the 1980s, the GDR increased trade with France and started to expand its trade with Japan, which could supply valuable new technology. Despite these increased trade relations with the West, however, trade with the United States remains minimal.

A fairly serious problem for the GDR is its lack of access to Western technology. The East Germans are still paying for millions of dollars' worth of Western European industrial equipment that they obtained on credit during the 1970s. Because they have not been able to sell many of their own products in the West, they have no hard Western currency with

In the past few years, East Germany's heavy industries have produced more machinery and automobiles.

which to purchase more Western equipment. And they cannot use their own currency for these purchases because the GDR-mark is not exchangeable for other currencies on the world market.

Transportation and Communications

Most of East Germany's transportation and communications equipment was destroyed in World War II, and what was not destroyed was confiscated by the Soviet Union after the war. The Soviets took trains and gasoline-powered vehicles and even uprooted railroad tracks for use in their own country.

It took a long time for the East Germans to repair or replace the railroads, highways, ports, and canals they lost to the war and the Russians. Finally, in the 1960s, the government started to expand the system of *autobahns*, or highways, that the GDR inherited from Nazi Germany. It completed construction of two major highways in the 1970s: one connecting Dresden and Leipzig, and the other linking East Berlin with the important port of Rostock. By 1980, the GDR had 72,872 miles (117,324 kilometers) of roads, more than twice as much as in 1972. Along with these new highways, the East German road system includes many secondary roads, most of which are paved and well maintained.

The GDR has a large equipment-manufacturing industry that produces cars, trucks, and buses. Although most citizens still use the GDR's extensive public transportation system, 43 percent of households owned automobiles as of 1984. As the average income of workers increases, so does the number of private automobiles on the road.

Rail and Air Services

The GDR's rebuilt railroad system includes 8,900 miles (14,329 kilometers) of track—one of the densest systems in Europe. Over the years, the government has replaced slow, steam-powered locomotives with efficient diesel and electric-powered trains. Newer and larger freight cars were also acquired to move bulk cargo. Today, railroads handle 70 percent of the country's cargo transport. The system's main junctions are at East Berlin, Leipzig, Dresden, Halle, and Magdeburg.

The railroads also move millions of passengers each year. Passenger lines include international train ferries—large boats with built-in train tracks that transport passenger trains across short stretches of the Baltic Sea and link them to rail systems on the opposite shore. One ferry links Rostock-Warnemunde to Gedser, in Denmark, and another connects the German coastal town of Sassnitz with Trelleborg, Sweden.

Interflug, the GDR's national airline, was founded in 1955 and gradually became an important freight transporter. Today, it moves more tons of freight than the GDR's inland waterways, once the country's most important form of transportation. Interflug also transports about 1.5 million

East Germany's railroads move millions of passengers each year. This rail station serves the city of Templin.

passengers per year. Over the years, it has gradually expanded its passenger service to other Eastern European Communist countries and beyond.

Waterways and Seaports

The GDR's system of inland waterways includes the Elbe River and the series of canals that connect it and its tributaries with the Oder and Neisse rivers. The system includes 1,564 miles (2,518 kilometers) of waterway, 1,081 miles (1,740 km) of which can be navigated by ships that weigh up to 100 tons (111 metric tons). Like the railroads, the inland waterways are especially important for the movement of bulk cargo, such as oil and grain. The most important link in this inland system is the port of Magdeburg, in the western GDR.

The commercial potential of the GDR's Baltic seacoast was neglected until the late 1950s, when the government decided to expand existing minor ports into major harbors and shipbuilding centers. Rostock became the most important port town, followed by Stralsund and Wismar. Together, these ports handle millions of tons of freight per year. Furthermore, many oceangoing ships, including more than 190 of the flag vessels in the East German merchant fleet, have been built in their shipyards.

Communications

Like other aspects of East German society, mass media are often used to advance the government's goals. East German newspapers, magazines, and radio and television stations emphasize the Socialist Unity party's viewpoint on all issues. Only stories approved by the party are reported in the media.

Because information is so strictly controlled, there are very few news outlets in the GDR. Deutscher Nachrichtendienst, the only news agency in East Germany, is owned and operated by the state. The East German press consists of only 40 daily newspapers (with a collective circulation of 7.5 million readers) and 27 periodicals, magazines, and weekly newspapers (with a collective circulation of 7 million).

East Germany's leading daily papers are published in East Berlin, Dresden, Leipzig, Karl Marx City, and Halle. The largest and most influential is East Berlin's *Neues Deutschland*. Circulated internationally, it presents the official SED view of East German affairs, including reports on the party's Central Committee meetings.

The government controls the broadcasting media through the State Broadcasting Committee, which was set up in 1952. East German television programs present cultural information and light entertainment as well as news. The GDR produces many of its own programs and imports others from its Communist neighbors. It was one of the first three countries to join Intervision, a television network that links Communist and Socialist states around the world via cable and satellite transmission.

East German broadcasters try to present interesting programs, because West German radio and television programs are also received throughout East Germany. Yet, despite dramatic improvements in the past few years, East German television remains unpopular. Most East Germans prefer to watch West German programs, which offer alternatives to the SED's version of current events. West German programs also offer East Germans a glimpse of the West, which they are forbidden to visit.

The Berliner Rundfunk, which serves East Berlin and its surrounding area, is the GDR's major radio station. Like East Germany's two other stations, it plays classical and popular music and presents educational programs. The radio services include an international station that transmits in more than a dozen languages to all parts of the world.

Today, modern automobiles drive down East Germany's ancient, cobblestoned streets. The country has preserved its historic past while building for the future.

The Challenge of the Future

East Germany faced difficult challenges long before it became a separate nation in 1949. Its history is one of violent clashes. Many of the world's most fearsome military leaders—Caesar, Charlemagne, Napoleon, and others—battled for control of the East German countryside at some time during their careers. Yet, despite its bloody past, Germany has managed to produce many of history's greatest artists, writers, musicians, and philosophers, including Martin Luther, Goethe, Haydn, and Bach.

Today, as the German Democratic Republic, East Germany continues to thrive despite adversity. The partitioning of Germany, intended as a temporary measure, has become a permanent split. Germans on both sides of the border share a common culture and heritage, but they are cut off from one another. It took many East Germans a long time to adjust to this separation and the new way of life that accompanied it. But over the past 40 years, most have stopped thinking of themselves as "second-class" Germans and have accepted the Communist system that was forced on them.

The GDR is an authoritarian state. The Socialist Unity party (SED) dominates its political system, and all power rests with its leadership. But despite its authoritarian nature, the government also serves the well-being of most of its citizens. Today, the GDR has a higher standard of living than any other country in the Communist bloc—including the Soviet Union. It has excellent health care and educational systems. Housing is inexpensive and widely available, and modern consumer goods are becoming more available as the economy continues to expand.

The GDR is the world's tenth most productive industrial power and an important producer of heavy machinery, chemicals, and microelectronic units. Industry accounts for about 70 percent of the national income and employs more than 40 percent of the work force. Agricultural production is growing, even though the number of people employed in agriculture is decreasing.

Almost everyone in the country can read and write, and almost everyone of working age either has a job or attends college. More than 60 percent of industrial employees are skilled workers, and at least 30 percent are college or technical school graduates. The most gifted and best-educated citizens are part of the GDR's technical intelligentsia—engineers, scientists, and bureaucrats who plot the country's economic and political future.

Women, who account for 50 percent of the GDR's work force, receive equal pay for equal work. The state provides married women and mothers with educational opportunities and free day care for their children. And, although it encourages large families, the government also provides free contraception and allows abortions.

The GDR's birthrate has increased slightly since the 1970s, but its death rate remains high because of the population's abnormally high percentage of older people. Part of the challenge of the future is to maintain economic growth in the face of a steadily shrinking work force. The government is hoping to meet that challenge by building an increasingly efficient economy.

To accomplish this goal, the GDR must improve the quality of its products so that it can compete for larger markets in the non-Communist world. Increased sales in the West would provide the GDR with the cash it needs to purchase advanced industrial machinery from the West. As the government is beginning to realize, the GDR's economy cannot continue to grow without the latest equipment.

In the near future, the GDR will remain tied to the Soviet Union and to other fellow members of the Council for Mutual Economic Assistance. In the long run, however, the GDR may have to loosen its ties to the Soviets if it is to become the independent nation-state that its leaders intend it to be.

The East German government has proved that is possible to build a productive Communist state. Its people are recognized as some of the most industrious and best educated in the world. The country produces world-class athletes, and many of its technological achievements rival those of Western nations. But it also represses art and literature, restricts its citizens' freedoms, and forbids travel outside the country.

The German Democratic Republic is a 40-year-old nation, but its history is 3,000 years long. It has faced turmoil and repression many times before, but it has always triumphed, both culturally and intellectually. The East German people proudly carry on this tradition.

◄ G L O S S A R Y ►

Autobahn   A high-speed roadway.

Baroque   A style of art that flourished in Europe from the 16th through the 18th centuries. Its chief characteristic is a great amount of elaborate decoration.

Blitzkrieg   "Lightning war," the term used to describe quick, forceful raids carried out by aircraft, tanks, and infantry during World War II.

Jugendweihe   The ceremony of initiation into adulthood and political activity, usually on the fourteenth birthday. This and other ceremonies have been created to replace older religious traditions, which the state discourages.

Kaiser   The title of the Prussian emperor. It is related to the imperial titles *caesar* (Roman) and *czar* (Russian).

Limes   The 3,000-mile (4,830-kilometer) series of fortifications built by the Romans in the 1st century B.C. to guard the frontier between the Roman and Germanic empires.

Nazi   A member of the National Socialist party, which came to power under Adolf Hitler in 1933.

Particularism   The practice by local princes of seeking power for themselves and their small states instead of supporting the German kingdom. This policy weakened Germany from the Middle Ages to the 19th century.

Reformation   The period of religious revolution started in 1517 by Martin Luther, who wanted to rid the Roman Catholic church of practices he believed were corrupt. The Reformation eventually gave birth to the Protestant Christian sects.

◄ I N D E X ►

I

industry 79–81, 90
Investiture Controversy 31

J

Jews 13, 39, 57, 59
judicial system 76
Jugendweihe 60, 92

K

kaiser 13, 37, 92

L

lakes 22
language 9, 62
limes 27, 92
Luther, Martin 12, 17, 32–33, 71, 89
Luxemburg family 32

M

marriage 57, 59
mass organizations 75–76

N

Napoleonic Wars 12
Nazis (National Socialists) 13, 39, 40,
   52, 84, 92
Neisse River 21, 52, 86

O

Oder River 21, 22, 27, 52, 82, 86
Ore Mountains 21, 22

P

particularism 29, 92
plant life 23–25
population 9, 57, 65, 67, 68, 71

Protestantism 12, 32–33, 59
Prussia 12, 13, 34, 36, 38

R

rainfall 23
Reformation 32–33, 92
Renaissance 19, 32–34
Rhine River 11, 27
rivers 22
Roman Catholic church 31, 32–33, 59
Roman Empire 11, 19, 27 (see also
   Holy Roman Empire)
Russia (see Soviet Union)

S

Salian Dynasty 12, 31
Second Reich 37
Socialist Unity party (SED) 53–55, 57,
   61, 73–75, 89
Soviet Union 13, 14, 17–18, 19, 37,
   38, 40, 49, 51, 52–53, 55, 76, 77,
   82, 84, 90, 91
sports 62–63

T

Third Reich 13, 40, 49
Thirty Years' War 12, 33–34
Thüringer Wald 22
trade 19, 82–84
transportation 84–86
tribes 11, 17, 27–28, 57

U

United Nations 14
United States 13–14, 17, 38, 40, 49,
   51, 83

W

Wagner, Richard 17, 69
Weimar Republic 13, 38–39

ACKNOWLEDGMENTS

The author and publisher are grateful to the following sources for photographs: ADN/Zentralbild (pp. 30, 50, 56, 63, 75, 77); American Red Cross (p. 49); Renate Hellmann (pp. 42, 43b); Ellen S. Knudsen (pp. 42-43, 43a, 44a, 44b, 45a, 46-47, 48a, 48b); Library of Congress (pp. 26, 34, 37, 41, 54, 58, 60, 64, 69, 70); National Lutheran Council (pp. 33, 39); Pan Am (p. 52); H. Armstrong Roberts (cover photo); Renata and Martin Stein (pp. 16, 18, 20, 23, 61, 66, 68, 72, 81, 83, 85, 88); Janice Wenger (pp. 45b, 48c); Bob Willis (p. 2); World Wildlife Fund (p. 24). Picture editor: Marty Baldessari. Picture research: Willa Percival.